THE ULTIMATE PUB QUIZ BOOK

500 Questions on General Knowledge

Compiled by

Scott Stevenson

First published in 2015 by
Apex Publishing Ltd
12A St. John's Road, Clacton on Sea
Essex, CO15 4BP, United Kingdom
www.apexpublishing.co.uk

Typesetting and layout by
Andrews UK Limited
www.andrewsuk.com

Cover design: Hannah Blamires

Cover models: Edward Burley, Chris
Cowlin and Mark Goddard

Contents

About The Author

Scott Stevenson is an actor, author and artist. He was born in Bath in 1983 and grew up in rural surroundings, close to the Mendip Hills. He has a 2:1 bachelor degree in Environmental Science from Bath Spa University.

After spending a number of years managing a team supporting children and young adults on the autistic spectrum, Scott followed his dream of working in the film and television industry. To date he has appeared in nearly 200 productions including featured roles in commercially successful movies such as *Les Misérables, Muppets Most Wanted, Mission: Impossible 5* and *The Imitation Game* and well-loved television series, most notably *Doctor Who, Downton Abbey* and *EastEnders* to name but a few.

Scott also paints commissioned artwork, writes children's stories and likes to watch his beloved Liverpool FC play. He also participates in local pub quizzes across Somerset and frequently composes quiz questions for social functions – a pastime which has led to him publishing quizzes for quizmasters across the country.

Scott lives in Midsomer Norton, in Somerset, where he enjoys spending time with his young family.

Foreword by Chris Cowlin

We all watch television and see so many quiz-based shows asking general knowledge questions and most of us can't resist shouting at the TV with an answer – sometimes the right one and, perhaps more often, the wrong one. Whatever your success rate in answering questions, one thing is clear; we all enjoy a good quiz.

I first met the author of this book, Scott Stevenson, on the set of a TV production and I was surprised by his broad general knowledge. For fun, while we waiting to be called on set, I tested him on some of the quiz books I have written and he fared very well, so I challenged him to write one himself.

Scott was certainly more than up to the task. He is a quiz fanatic and regularly takes part in pub quizzes in and around Somerset, where he lives, as well as compiling questions for quiz masters. This book has been thoroughly researched by Scott for you, your friends and family to enjoy and the 500 thought-provoking questions have been carefully designed to get you thinking.

Covering a range of different subjects, from art and literature through to sport and geography, as well as a 'name the year' section, there is something to suit all abilities and ages. So whether you are a budding genius or simply curious about the world we live in, this book is sure to both entertain and inform.

Chris Cowlin
Best-selling quiz book author
www.chriscowlin.co.uk

Introduction

With 500 carefully composed, pub quiz style questions, the content of this quiz book should appeal to quizzers of all abilities. Not only that, with ten subjects each containing fifty questions, quiz masters have five ready-made quiz nights to bring the punters in! If you're having a social gathering and want to test your family and friends or just want to brush up on your own general knowledge then this book is a handy addition to your quiz book collection.

Happy quizzing!
Scott Stevenson

THE ULTIMATE PUB
QUIZ BOOK

Questions – Art and Literature

1. *The Scream* is the name of each of the four versions of a compilation created using paint and pastels between 1893 and 1910 by which expressionist artist?

2. The play *Shadowlands* is based on the relationship between American writer Joy Gresham and which Belfast-born poet and novelist?

3. Emma Thompson won a Golden Globe Award for her role in a TV adaptation of which Jane Austen novel?

4. Which famous English poet was a volunteer in Greece's War of Independence in the early 19th century?

5. Whose novel *Trainspotting*, published in 1993, later achieved cult status due to the Danny Boyle-directed film based on it?

6. Which author and politician with the middle name Rodham wrote *Living History*?

7. Who wrote the book *All Creatures Great and Small*?

8. Published in 1982, Alice Walker's Pulitzer Prize-winning novel features what colour in its title?

9. In a series of children's books by Lauren Child, what is the name of seven-year old Charlie's little sister?

10. In 1999, which British artist was nominated for the Turner Prize for her piece *My Bed*?

11. In David Hockney's painting, *Mr and Mrs Clark and Percy,* what animal is Percy?

12. In what country did Tintin first appear in print?

13. What was Emily Bronte's only published novel?

14. Which Ian McEwan novel was adapted into a 2007 film starring Keira Knightley?

15. Who wrote *Moby Dick*?

16. What does the 'S' in author C.S. Lewis's name stand for?

17. In *Julius Caeser*, how did Mark Anthony die?

18. Who wrote *Utopia* published in 1516?

19. In Robert Louis Stevenson's *Treasure Island* how many men are there on a 'dead man's chest'?

20. Which ballet features the *Waltz of the Snowflakes*?

21. What comic book publishers created the characters Green Goblin and Red Skull?

22. Which author served as a physician in the Second Boer War?

23. In the novel by E.M. Forster, what is 'Howard's End'?

24. What is the subject of Ernest Hemmingway's book *Death in the Afternoon*?

25. Who wrote *Les Misérables*, first published in 1862?

26. Who created the fictional character Adrian Mole?

27. Which British novelist also writes under the pseudonym Robert Galbraith?

28. Which famous artist frequently travelled with a pet ocelot called Babou?

29. Who was the first poet to be buried in 'Poet's Corner' in Westminster Abbey?

30. Who wrote the short story *The Canterville Ghost*?

31. Who created the characters 'Rabbit', 'Piglet' and 'Owl'?

32. Who painted *The Night Watch* in 1642?

33. Who wrote *Three Men in a Boat* in 1889?

34. The name of which artist appears in the title of a Dan Brown novel?

35. According to folklore, Will Scarlet was a member of which notorious outlaw's gang?

36. William Shakespeare's *Hamlet* was set in which country?

37. Oceania is the fictional setting for which George Orwell novel published in 1949?

38. What is the name of the fictional village in the long-running British radio soap opera *The Archers*?

39. *West Side Story*, based on Shakespeare's play *Romeo and Juliet* featured which two rival gangs?

40. Who wrote the fairy tale *The Ugly Duckling*?

41. What is the name of the owl given to Harry Potter on his eleventh birthday in the Harry Potter series of books?

42. *Corner of the Garden at Montgeron* is a 19th century painting by which impressionist?

43. Which singer's life story, *Autobiography* was published by Penguin Classics in 2013?

44. Which French artist and sculptor created works including *The Kiss* and *The Thinker*?

45. Which Julia Donaldson book telling the story of a mouse's journey through the woods has sold over thirteen million copies, has won several prizes for children's literature and has been developed into plays on both the West End and Broadway?

46. Which author coined the nonsense word 'mimsy' by combining the words 'flimsy' and 'miserable' in his poem *Jabberwocky*?

47. Who wrote the book *Dracula*?

48. What is the literal translation of Adolf Hitler's autobiographical manifesto *Mein Kampf* published in 1925?

49. Who famously wrote, 'I can resist anything, except temptation'?

50. Who wrote the 1924 novel *A Passage to India*?

Answers – Art and Literature

1. Edvard Munch

2. C. S. Lewis

3. *Sense and Sensibility*

4. Lord Byron

5. Irvine Welsh

6. Hillary Clinton

7. James Herriot

8. Purple (*The Color Purple*)

9. Lola

10. Tracey Emin

11. A cat

12. Belgium

13. *Wuthering Heights*

14. *Atonement*

15. Herman Melville

16. Staples

17. He fell on his own sword

18. Sir Thomas More

19. Fifteen

20. *The Nutcracker*

21. Marvel

22. Sir Arthur Conan Doyle

23. A house

24. Bullfighting

25. Victor Hugo

26. Sue Townsend

27. J. K. Rowling

28. Salvador Dali

29. Geoffrey Chaucer

30. Oscar Wilde

31. A. A. Milne

32. Rembrandt

33. Jerome K. Jerome

34. Leonardo da Vinci (*The Da Vinci Code*)

35. Robin Hood's

36. Denmark

37. *Nineteen Eighty-Four*

38. Ambridge

Questions – Geography

51. Erosion by which river, is thought by geologists to have formed the Grand Canyon?

52. With a population of 1.5 million and lying on the banks of the Mtkvari River, what is the capital and largest city of eastern European country Georgia?

53. What is the only US state named after an English county?

54. What African country lies directly to the north of Namibia?

55. Which gemstone, the largest of its kind, was mined in Sri Lanka and known as 'The Star of India'?

56. Cagliari is the capital city of which island?

57. Gower and Iberian are examples of which geographical feature?

58. What Scandinavian country obtained independence from Russia in 1917?

59. What is the only American state whose name consists of only one syllable?

60. What does the 'Q' stand for in the Australian airlines acronym QANTAS?

61. What was the capital city of the USA before Washington, DC?

62. What mountain overlooks Cape Town in South Africa?

63. What desert did David Livingstone famously cross in 1849?

64. What is the largest island of the Inner Hebrides?

65. Which City in the UK has the shortest name?

66. George Washington, Abraham Lincoln and Thomas Jefferson are three of the United States' presidents immortalised in the Mount Rushmore monument. Who is the fourth?

67. What is the smallest country on mainland Africa?

68. In which ocean is Fiji located?

69. On what river are the 'Victoria Falls'?

70. The Andaman Sea forms part of which ocean?

71. Raki is an alcoholic beverage from which country?

72. In which London street is the Bank of England located?

73. In which UK city is Strangeways prison?

74. Cambria is an old name for which country?

75. Which Australian state has the biggest population?

76. What nationality was Christopher Columbus?

77. In which country is 'Angel Falls', the world's highest waterfall?

78. For what was Gerardus Mercator famous in the 16th century?

79. What city in Hertfordshire was founded on the site of the martyrdom of the saint it is named after?

80. On what Mediterranean island are the 'Venetian Stairs' and the 'Blue Grotto'?

81. In which Northern Irish county is the Giant's Causeway?

82. What is the only US State with two vowels as the first two letters?

83. What country sends Britain a Christmas tree each year to erect in Trafalgar Square?

84. What were there thirteen of in 1776 and now there are fifty of?

85. In which European city are the Tivoli Gardens?

86. In South America what is a 'pampero'?

87. What Scottish mountain range separates The Highlands from The Lowlands?

88. In which English county would you find Stonehenge?

89. Vietnam gained independence from which country in 1954?

90. Mongolia is the only country whose capital begins with what letter?

91. In what US city could you see 'The Liberty Bell'?

92. In what country is the city of Gothenburg?

93. The 'Rosetta Stone' currently in the British Museum, came from which country?

94. In what city is the Anne Frank museum?

95. What is the name of the small island which sits at the top of Niagara Falls?

96. The Bass Strait separates Australia from which land mass?

97. What is the name of the only city in Cornwall?

98. What is the only African country whose English name has only one syllable?

99. Addis Ababa, meaning 'New Flower' is the capital city of which country?

100. Which city in the UK is home to the largest clock face?

Answers – Geography

51. Colorado

52. Tblisi

53. New Hampshire

54. Angola

55. Sapphire

56. Sardinia

57. Peninsula

58. Finland

59. Maine

60. Queensland

61. Philadelphia

62. Table Mountain

63. Kalahari

64. Skye

65. Ely

66. Theodore Roosevelt

67. The Gambia

68. Pacific Ocean

69.   Zambezi

70.   Indian Ocean

71.   Turkey

72.   Threadneedle Street

73.   Manchester

74.   Wales

75.   New South Wales

76.   Italian

77.   Venezuela

78.   Map making

79.   Saint Albans

80.   Capri

81.   County Antrim

82.   Iowa

83.   Norway

84.   American States

85.   Copenhagen

86.   A dry wind

87.   The Grampions

88.   Wiltshire

89. France

90. U (Ulan Bator)

91. Philadelphia

92. Sweden

93. Egypt

94. Amsterdam

95. Goat Island

96. Tasmania

97. Truro

98. Chad

99. Ethiopia

100. Liverpool (Liver Building)

Questions – Name The Year

101.   Scientist and inventor Barnes Wallis used his 'bouncing bomb' in action for the first time, Rodgers and Hammerstein's stage musical *Oklahoma!* opens on Broadway and Mick Jagger was born.

102.   Queen Elizabeth The Queen Mother was born, football clubs Lazio and FC Bayern Munich are established and British soldiers invade Pretoria in the Second Boer War.

103.   Plane crash that ended the lives of promising young musicians Buddy Holly, Ritchie Valens and 'The Big Bopper', Alaska is admitted as the 49th US state and actors Hugh Laurie and Kevin Spacey are born.

104.   Robert Falcon Scott and his team reach the South Pole, the *RMS Titanic* strikes an iceberg and sinks killing 1517 people and American artist Jackson Pollock is born.

105.   US President Abraham Lincoln was assassinated at Ford's theatre in Washington, DC by actor John Wilkes Booth, John Deere receives patent for ploughs and the first speed limit is introduced in Britain: two mph in towns and four mph in the country.

106.   Frankie Howerd dies the day before fellow comedian Benny Hill, Disneyland Paris (formally Euro Disney) opens and a fire breaks out at Windsor Castle. This year was subsequently labelled 'annus horribilis' by Queen Elizabeth II.

107.   The BBC was founded, Benito Mussolini becomes the youngest ever Prime Minister of Italy aged thirty-nine and American actress and singer Doris Day is born.

108. Singer Michael Jackson dies, Slovakia adopts the euro as its national currency and Air France Flight 447 crashes into the Atlantic Ocean, killing all 228 passengers.

109. Arthur Wellesley, 1st Duke of Wellington beats Napoleon at the Battle of Waterloo, Louis XVIII returns to Paris and becomes King of France and Luxembourg declares independence from the French Empire.

110. The Great Fire of London breaks out on Pudding Lane destroying more than 13,000 buildings and killing just six people, Isaac Newton discovers the laws of gravitation and uses a prism to spilt sunlight into the component colours of the optical spectrum. This year also contains all of the Roman Numerals used only once in order from biggest to smallest (MDCLXVI).

111. Concorde takes its first commercial flight, Summer Olympics are held in Montreal and Winter Olympic Games are held in Innsbruck, Austria.

112. Haiti is devastated by an earthquake, air traffic is disrupted across northern and western Europe following the eruption of an Icelandic volcano which produced extensive ash clouds and thirty-three Chilean miners are safely rescued after being trapped underground for sixty-nine days.

113. Halley's Comet can be seen from Earth (stargazers will have to wait seventy-six years before seeing it again), George V becomes King of England and American outlaw Bonnie Parker is born.

114. Dwight D. Eisenhower becomes the 34th President of the United States, Sir Edmund Hillary and Tenzing Norgay become the first climbers to reach the summit of Mount Everest and Hugh Hefner publishes the first issue of *Playboy*.

115. Edward the Confessor of York dies and Harold II is crowned King of England but dies in battle just months later. This year is traditionally known as the end of the Dark Ages.

116. 'Decimal Day' occurs in the UK, Jackie Stewart wins the Monaco Grand Prix and the first Reading Music Festival takes place.

117. The *General Belgrano* is sunk during the Falklands conflict, the FIFA World Cup is held in Spain and Michael Jackson releases the album *Thriller*.

118. James Dean dies aged twenty-four after a car crash in California, Jim Henson creates his first version of Kermit the Frog and Winston Churchill resigns as Prime Minister aged eighty.

119. Elvis Presley is born, Porky Pig makes debut as the first major Looney Tunes character and Persia is renamed Iran.

120. Osama bin Laden is killed in Pakistan, Anders Breivik kills seventy-seven people in twin terror attacks in Norway and Steve Jobs, co-founder and CEO of Apple dies after cancer battle.

121. Tony Blair becomes Prime Minister, Channel 5 is launched in the UK and Hong Kong obtains independence from Great Britain.

122. Richard Nixon resigns following the Watergate scandal, ABBA win Eurovision Song Contest with 'Waterloo' and Muhammad Ali knocks out George Foreman in Zaire in a fight billed as 'The Rumble in the Jungle'.

123. A flash flood causes extensive damage to the Cornish village of Boscastle and a Boxing Day earthquake off the coast of Indonesia leads to a tsunami, which kills over

230,000 people in fourteen countries including Thailand, India and Sri Lanka.

124.   Playwright William Shakespeare dies, English explorer Sir Walter Raleigh is released from prison and Ben Jonson becomes second poet laureate, appointed by James I. This year also comprises of just two different digits.

125.   The thirteen colonies of North America (now known as the United States of America) declare independence from the British Empire, Captain James Cook sets off from Plymouth to the Pacific Ocean on his final doomed voyage and George III acknowledges that the war against the United States isn't going too well in a speech to parliament.

126.   Queen Victoria is born, Thomas Jefferson founds the University of Virginia and Scottish inventor James Watt dies.

127.   The BBC broadcasts the first episode of *Doctor Who*, The Beatles record their debut album *Please Please Me* in a single day at the Abbey Road Studios and The Great Train Robbery takes place in Buckinghamshire.

128.   The first episode of *EastEnders* is shown in the UK and *Neighbours* airs for the first time in Australia, Greenpeace vessel Rainbow Warrior is sunk in Auckland Harbour, British Formula One driver Lewis Hamilton is born and Live Aid, the dual venue concert organised by Bob Geldof, raising money for the Ethiopian famine takes place.

129.   The Hillsborough disaster claims the lives of ninety-six Liverpool supporters, the Berlin wall is torn down and France celebrates the 200th anniversary of the French Revolution.

130. Red Rum wins his first Grand National, Spanish artist Pablo Picasso dies in France and Princess Anne marries Captain Mark Phillips in Westminster Abbey.

131. Johnny Wilkinson's drop goal against Australia wins England the Rugby World Cup, US forces seize control of Baghdad, ending Saddam Hussein's regime and actor Bob Hope dies.

132. Mel Gibson's *Braveheart* is released, O.J. Simpson is found not guilty of double murder, Rose West is sentenced to life in prison for killing ten females and *Toy Story*, the first-ever full length computer animated feature film is released.

133. Three-time Formula One world champion Ayrton Senna is killed in an accident during the San Marino Grand Prix, The Channel Tunnel, which took 15,000 workers and seven years to complete, opens and the FIFA World Cup is held in the United States.

134. Charlie Chaplin's remains are stolen, Pope John Paul I and Pope John Paul II become Pope and Louise Brown is the first baby to be born after conception by In Vitro Fertilisation (IVF).

135. *Home and Away* premieres in Australia, the Summer Olympic Games are held in Seoul, South Korea and Pan Am flight 103 crashes in Lockerbie, Scotland following a terrorist bombing.

136. Queen Elizabeth II celebrates her Diamond Jubilee, protester Trenton Oldfield temporarily halts the Oxford and Cambridge boat race by jumping into the River Thames and swimming between the two boats and Felix Baumgartner becomes the first person to break the sound barrier without any machine assistance during a record space dive twenty-four miles above the Earth.

137. Daley Thompson wins his first Decathlon gold at the Summer Olympic Games in Moscow, *Star Wars Episode V: The Empire Strikes Back* is released and John Lennon is assassinated by Mark Chapman in New York.

138. Wikipedia, the virtual encyclopaedia goes online, George W. Bush is sworn into office succeeding Bill Clinton as President of the United States and John Prescott punches farmer Craig Evans in Rhyl, North Wales during the Labour election campaign.

139. A group of Islamic extremist suicide bombers attack underground lines and a double-decker bus in London, killing fifty-two people, over four million people travel to the Vatican to mourn the death of Pope John Paul II and Marcus Luttrell is the sole Navy Seal survivor of Operation Red Wings which was later portrayed in the film *Lone Survivor* starring Mark Wahlberg.

140. Malaysian Airlines flight MH370 goes missing after leaving Kuala Lumpur airport on route to Beijing, Uruguayan footballer Luis Suarez is banned for nine international matches after biting the shoulder of Italian defender Georgio Chiellini, the Ebola virus kills over 10,000 people in West Africa and the Winter Olympic Games are held in Sochi, Russia.

141. '(I can't get no) satisfaction' by The Rolling Stones reaches number one in the UK and the USA, the state funeral of Sir Winston Churchill takes place in London and English footballer Sir Stanley Matthews plays his final First Division game aged fifty years and five days.

142. Adolf Hitler becomes leader of Germany, *Doctor Who* actor Tom Baker is born and Italy beat Czechoslovakia in extra time to win the FIFA World Cup.

143. Space Shuttle Challenger makes its first flight, The Jules Rimet Trophy is stolen in Rio de Janeiro and singer Amy Winehouse is born.

144. Anne Frank dies of typhus in the Bergen-Belsen concentration camp in Germany, Eva Braun commits suicide in a Berlin bunker and British rock singer Rod Stewart is born.

145. Amy Johnson becomes the first woman to fly solo from England to Australia, the first FIFA World Cup is held in Uruguay and actor and director Clint Eastwood is born.

146. Queen Victoria dies aged eighty-one after more than sixty-three years on the throne, Guglielmo Marconi receives the first trans-Atlantic radio signal and American Jazz musician Louis Armstrong is born.

147. The Summer Olympic Games are held in Sydney, Australia, English actor and writer Sir Alec Guinness dies and Vladamir Putin is elected President of Russia.

148. Rupert Murdoch purchases *The News of the World*, the largest selling British Sunday newspaper, Formula One ace Michael Schumacher is born and photographer Iain Macmillan takes a photograph of The Beatles on a zebra crossing on Abbey Road.

149. *Titanic* wins eleven Oscars including Best Picture at the 70th Academy Awards ceremony, Bear Grylls becomes the youngest British climber to scale Mount Everest, aged twenty-three and American entertainer Frank Sinatra dies.

150. Welsh comedian and magician Tommy Cooper is born, The United States formally ends World War I years after the last combat action and White Castle Hamburger, the world's first fast food chain, opens in Wichita, Kansas.

Answers – Name The Year

101.   1943

102.   1900

103.   1959

104.   1912

105.   1865

106.   1992

107.   1922

108.   2009

109.   1815

110.   1066

111.   1976

112.   2010

113.   1910

114.   1953

115.   1066

116.   1971

117.   1982

118.   1955

119.   1935

120.   2011

121.   1997

122.   1974

123.   2004

124.   1616

125.   1776

126.   1819

127.   1963

128.   1985

129.   1989

130.   1973

131.   2003

132.   1995

133.   1994

134.   1978

135.   1988

136.   2012

137.   1980

138.   2001

139. 2005

140. 2014

141. 1965

142. 1934

143. 1983

144. 1945

145. 1930

146. 1901

147. 2000

148. 1969

149. 1998

150. 1921

Questions – Animals

151. Humans are the only primates to not have what on the palms of their hands?

152. What is the collective noun given to a group of owls?

153. What is the fastest two-legged land animal?

154. What part of their bodies do butterflies taste with?

155. On Christmas Day 2007, what animal escaped from San Francisco Zoo, killing a visitor?

156. Which creature is said to turn when a tolerant person eventually loses their patience?

157. What is the largest fish in the world?

158. What creature is an ophidiophobe afraid of?

159. What animal did the Aztecs refer to as a 'turtle rabbit'?

160. Which insect gives its name to a street market that sells second hand goods?

161. What is the UK's smallest bird of prey?

162. The sparkling is a species of which type of insect?

163. With what animal would a hostler work?

164. The common magpie has what colour beak?

165. A decapod is a crustacean with how many pairs of legs?

166. What is the collective term for the number of eggs laid by a bird?

167. What is a young swan called?

168. What animal lives in a 'Holt'?

169. Brazilian, Malayan, Baird's, Kabomani and Mountain are species of which endangered herbivorous mammal, similar in shape to a pig with a prehensile snout?

170. Sacred to the ancient Egyptians, what creature was a scarab?

171. The 'lesser great leaf-nosed' and 'lesser horseshoe' are what kind of creatures?

172. What type of ancient animal was a 'Mastodon'?

173. What animal provides fifty per cent of all the protein for food in Peru?

174. What is the common term for a female alligator?

175. As canine relates to dogs, 'murine' relates to what animal?

176. A gnu is another name for which animal?

177. Where does a horse have 'frogs'?

178. 'The Queen of Spain', 'Green Hairstreak' and 'Monarch' are species of what creature?

179. What mammal's name derives from the Malay and Indonesian term for 'person of the forest'?

180. Hamsters belong to what order of mammals?

181. What mythical term is more commonly used when referring to the Komodo monitor lizard?

182. What sort of animal is a 'fennec'?

183. What colour is an adult female blackbird?

184. What name is given to the young of a beaver?

185. Arboreal animals are those living in which type of habitat?

186. What was the name of the first dog in space?

187. Sobek the Egyptian God usually manifests himself as a human with the head of which animal?

188. What type of animal is a 'mandrill'?

189. What is the correct name for a mature female cat?

190. What creature is an 'Australian Sea Wasp'?

191. What animal is the largest of the cat species?

192. When Spanish explorers discovered a group of islands 600 miles off the coast of Ecuador in the 16th century, they named them 'Galapago' which is a literal translation of which animal?

193. Brindle is a colouring of a dog's what?

194. The Bilby is an animal native to which country?

195. How many feet does a sloth have?

196. Reed, Marsh and Sedge are varieties of which bird?

197. What type of creature was Gub-Gub in the *Dr Dolittle* stories?

198. In the wild, which mammal pollinates banana plants?

199. Which fish are members of the class Asteroidea?

200. A Chilean pine tree, is more commonly called what?

Answers – Animals

151. Pigment

152. Parliament

153. Ostrich

154. Their feet

155. Tiger

156. A worm

157. Whale shark

158. Snakes

159. Armadillo

160. Flea

161. Merlin

162. Beetle

163. Horses

164. Black

165. Five

166. Clutch

167. Cygnet

168. Otter

169. A tapir

170. A beetle

171. Bats

172. Elephant

173. The Guinea Pig

174. Cow

175. Mouse

176. Wildebeest

177. On its hooves

178. Butterfly

179. Orangutan

180. Rodents

181. Dragon

182. A fox

183. Brown

184. A kitten

185. Trees

186. Laika

187. Crocodile

188. A monkey

189. A Queen

190. A jellyfish

191. Tiger

192. Tortoise

193. Coat

194. Australia

195. Four

196. Warbler

197. Pig

198. Bat

199. Starfish

200. Monkey puzzle/monkey tail tree

Questions – Sport

201. In what sport was Dan Maskell a professional, before becoming better known as a television and radio commentator?

202. What football club is former British Prime Minister Tony Blair known to be a fan of?

203. What object sits on top of the Wimbledon men's singles champion trophy and has done since 1887?

204. Katarina Johnson-Thompson is an Olympic athlete who specialises in what event?

205. In which sport often labelled 'The Fastest Game on Earth' is play allowed behind the netted goals?

206. Former England netball player Tracey Neville is the twin sister of which footballer?

207. In which Swiss city are the headquarters of FIFA?

208. How many players make up an Olympic curling team?

209. The phrase 'step up to the plate' originated from which sport?

210. Which town has been the headquarters for horse racing in England since the 17th century?

211. On a standard dart board, what is the lowest number that cannot be scored with a single dart?

212. Between 2004 and 2009, which player lost three Wimbledon singles finals, each time to Roger Federer?

213. From 2011 to 2013, the winning FA Cup managers all shared which first name?

214. Which is the lightest in weight, of the objects thrown in athletics field events?

215. What animals are the Argentina international rugby union team named after?

216. Which national football team was the first to win the World Cup four times?

217. What is known as the sport of kings?

218. In motorcycling, where do the TT races take place?

219. Which sport has a playing surface measuring 9 feet by 5 feet?

220. On 6 February 1971, where was a golf ball hit for the first time?

221. Which ex-policeman became a World Champion ice skater?

222. Which sporting event first took place in 1829?

223. What sport uses the terms 'tickle the kitty', 'tuck in' and 'blocker'?

224. Which is the longest track event in the decathlon?

225. In what city did Roger Bannister break the four-minute mile in 1954?

226. What is the maximum score that can be achieved in a game of ten-pin bowling?

227. What colour are the polka dots on the 'King of the Mountains' jersey worn in the Tour De France?

228. In what sport do teams compete for the 'Iroquois Cup'?

229. On a racing card, what does 'SP' stand for?

230. What rugby league forward who had played for England and Great Britain switched sports to rugby union and joined Bath in 2014?

231. Five Football teams beginning with the letter 'W' have played over 300 games in English football's top flight. West Ham and West Bromwich Albion are two, name the other three?

232. What card game has the same name as an English racecourse?

233. Which football team won the European Champions League in 2005?

234. 'Foil' and 'Sabre' are terms used in what sport?

235. How many stones are used by each team in a standard game of curling?

236. What do the French refer to as a 'Hippodrome'?

237. What footballer has played for Arsenal, Chelsea, Liverpool, Manchester City, Real Madrid and Paris Saint-Germain?

238. In what sport does the referee always wear gloves?

239. A statue of which 1930s' British tennis champion stands inside the main gates at Wimbledon?

240. The Tokyo Sevens is a tournament in what sport?

241. George W. Bush was once a co-owner of which US Baseball team?

242. How many points is the outer-bull worth in darts?

243. Which Irish international goalkeeper played in Mexico on his 21st and 41st birthday?

244. In 2011, a Formula One race was held in which country for the first time?

245. Who won the men's singles title at Wimbledon in 1985 aged just seventeen?

246. In America, what word precedes hockey to differentiate it from ice hockey?

247. Aryton Senna and Alain Prost drove together for what Formula One team?

248. Which Australian cricketer was the first to score 300 twice in test matches?

249. What sporting trophy was stolen for a second time in 1983 and remains unrecovered?

250. In what city can you find the two English Football League grounds that are closest together?

Answers – Sport

201. Tennis

202. Newcastle

203. A pineapple

204. Heptathlon

205. Ice Hockey

206. Phil Neville

207. Zurich

208. Four

209. Baseball

210. Newmarket

211. 23

212. Andy Roddick

213. Roberto

214. Javelin

215. Pumas

216. Brazil

217. Horse Racing

218. Isle of Man

219. Table Tennis

220. Moon

221. Christopher Dean

222. The oxford and Cambridge boat race

223. Bowls

224. 1500 metres

225. Oxford

226. 300

227. Red

228. Lacrosse

229. Starting Price

230. Sam Burgess

231. Wimbledon, Wolverhampton Wanderers and Wigan

232. Newmarket

233. Liverpool

234. Fencing

235. Eight

236. A race course

237. Nicholas Anelka

238. Snooker

239. Fred Perry

240. Rugby Union

241. Texas Rangers

242. 25

243. Pat Jennings

244. India (Jaypee Group Circuit)

245. Boris Becker

246. Field

247. McLaren

248. Sir Donald Bradman

249. Jules Rimet Trophy (football World Cup trophy)

250. Nottingham (Nottingham Forest and Notts County – 0.26 miles)

Questions – History

251. Which former Ugandan dictator died in 2003?

252. What French-made missile is thought to have caused the most damage during the Falklands War?

253. Which Austrian-born French monarch was executed in Paris on 16 October 1793?

254. Russia declared war on which country on 8 February 1904, subsequently known as the first great war of the 20th century?

255. Which British Prime Minister became Lord Avon?

256. Who was British Prime Minister at the outbreak of World War II?

257. What American University was founded near Boston in 1636?

258. On 16 September 1620, Puritans left Plymouth for America on which ship?

259. In 1907 Robert Baden Powell started which organisation?

260. According to Homer, the Greek Goddess Aphrodite was the daughter of which God?

261. In what century was Joan of Arc born?

262. In what decade of the 20th century was the UK's National Health Service launched?

263. Which royal house followed the 'Tudors'?

264. According to the Catholic Church, Saints Anne and Joachim are the grandparents of whom?

265. What year was the battle of Waterloo?

266. In World War II, what country occupied the Channel Islands?

267. What bird was the emblem of ancient Athens and appeared on its coins?

268. In Ancient Egypt, death was the penalty for killing which animal?

269. In World War II, what happened on 7 December 1941?

270. According to Greek mythology, who was the first woman on Earth?

271. What ship left Boston for Genoa in 1872 and was found abandoned four weeks later?

272. Who was Prime Minister of Britain when Queen Elizabeth II came to the thrown?

273. Which King had been Prince of Wales for sixty years before his Coronation?

274. Which royal wedding took place on 30 July 2011?

275. According to Napoleon, what does an army march on?

276. In 1886, the Prince of Wales opened a road tunnel under which river?

277. Who died on Coniston Water in January 1967?

278. Which 'Age' came between the 'Stone Age' and the 'Iron Age'?

279. The women tried at Salem in Massachusetts in 1692 were accused of what?

280. Robert I of Scotland was also known by what name?

281. Who is said to have laid his coat across a muddy patch of ground for Queen Elizabeth I to walk over?

282. According to the *Bible*, who was raised from the dead by Jesus?

283. Who founded a training school for nurses in London in 1860?

284. Which King of England was the only legitimate son of Henry VIII?

285. What was the main cause of the American Civil War?

286. Who shot and killed Lee Harvey Oswald?

287. In which century was the gunpowder plot?

288. Ivan IV of Russia is more commonly known by what name?

289. 'Lazar Houses' were used to treat people with which condition?

290. Which skin-tight one-piece garment was named after France's most famous acrobat of the 19th century?

291. Of which Red Indian tripe was Geronimo the chief?

292. To whom was King Louis XVI of France married?

293. Between 1577 and 1580, who sailed around the world in the ship which started its journey called the *Pelican* and finished it as the *Golden Hind*?

294. Who opened the first of ninety homes for orphans in 1870 and had the slogan 'No destitute child ever refused admission'?

295. What famous department store opened in Oxford Street in London in 1909?

296. 'The Good Friday Agreement' was signed in 1998 in what city?

297. Henry VIII was buried in Windsor Castle along with which of his former wives?

298. From whose action does the phrase 'turning a blind eye' come from?

299. Emily, Sylvia and Christabel were leading suffragettes from the same family. What was their surname?

300. Who was England's first Tudor King?

Answers – History

251. Idi Amin

252. Exocet

253. Marie Antoinette

254. Japan

255. Anthony Eden

256. Neville Chamberlain

257. Harvard

258. *Mayflower*

259. The Boy Scouts

260. Zeus

261. 15th

262. 1940s

263. The Stuarts

264. Jesus

265. 1815

266. Germany

267. Owl

268. Cat

269. Attack on Pearl Harbour

270. Pandora

271. *Mary Celeste*

272. Sir Winston Churchill

273. Edward VII

274. The marriage of Zara Phillips and Mike Tindall

275. Its stomach

276. The Mersey

277. Donald Campbell

278. Bronze Age

279. Witchcraft

280. Robert the Bruce

281. Sir Walter Raleigh

282. Lazarus

283. Florence Nightingale

284. Edward VI

285. Slavery

286. Jack Ruby

287. 17th

288. Ivan the Terrible

289. Leprosy

290. Leotard

291. Apachi

292. Marie Antionette

293. Sir Francis Drake

294. Dr Thomas Barnardo

295. Selfridges

296. Belfast

297. Jane Seymour

298. Lord Nelson

299. Pankhurst

300. Henry VII

Questions – Science

301. What chemical, used in the manufacture of toothpaste to prevent dental cavities was first used by 'Crest' in 1955?

302. 'Deglutition' is the medical term for which human biological process?

303. In 2001, which internal organ did doctors in New York City remove from a patient in Strasbourg, France, using remote controlled robots?

304. From which chemical element is coal derived?

305. What is the longest bone in the human body?

306. What type of acid would you find in a car battery?

307. 'Crescent', 'Gibbous', 'New' and 'Full' are phases of what?

308. What is the usual colour of copper sulphate?

309. Which vegetable, often used in a salad, is also known as a scallion?

310. The name of which fruit means 'apple having many seeds'?

311. Iron pyrite is also known by what name?

312. Which planet of the solar system has the shortest day?

313. What does the WD stand for in WD-40?

314. What are produced by the lacrimal glands?

315. In the human body which organ secretes the enzyme rennin?

316. What is the lightest known metal?

317. Which chemical element takes its name from the Greek word for 'colour'?

318. A 'Somnambulist' is someone who does what activity during the night?

319. A Campbell-Stokes recorder measures what?

320. What acid accumulates in the muscles once the anaerobic threshold is passed when doing exercise?

321. In the human body what is the medical name for the collar bone?

322. Pencil lead is mostly made from what substance?

323. What nerve forms the link between the eye and the brain?

324. What word is used to describe a wind represented by the number 12 on the 'Beaufort Scale'?

325. What effect does alcohol have on your body temperature?

326. Who founded the church of Scientology?

327. Of what metal is 'Maundy Money' made?

328. Relating to screens and monitors, what does LCD stand for?

329. What object did stargazers last see in 1986 and will next appear in 2061?

330. What is 'albumen'?

331. Which metal is commonly used as a shield against radiation?

332. Which gas has the chemical formula NH3?

333. What is the common name given to the thyroid cartilage projection at the front of the neck?

334. Which substances can be referred to as 'rare', 'noble', or 'inert'?

335. What was Apollo 11's landing module called?

336. What word is used to describe the rate at which the speed of an object increases?

337. Which part of the body would a chiropodist look after?

338. Hg is the chemical symbol for what metal?

339. In six billion years' time the Milky Way is predicted to merge with what other galaxy?

340. What is the name given to fossilised resin of coniferous trees from the Middle Tertiary period?

341. What is the main metal in the alloy bronze?

342. Arabica and robusta are the two most important commercial species of which plant?

343. What shapes are attached to a line of a weather map to denote a warm front?

344. What do 1,000 gigabytes make?

345. A speed record of 11.2mph was recorded where in 1972?

346. Although unsuccessful, which London structure was designed so it could act as a giant telescope?

347. Which acid is the base for vinegar?

348. What name is given to the condition which changes the colour of the skin due to too much bile in the bloodstream?

349. What is the brightest star in the night sky?

350. Which organs are affected by Bright's disease?

Answers – Science

301. Fluoride

302. Swallowing

303. Gall bladder

304. Carbon

305. Femur

306. Sulphuric or lead acid

307. The moon

308. Blue

309. Spring onion

310. Pomegranate

311. Fool's gold

312. Jupiter

313. Water Displacement

314. Tears

315. Kidneys

316. Lithium

317. Chromium

318. Sleep walks

319. Sunlight

320. Lactic acid

321. Clavicle

322. Graphite

323. Optic nerve

324. Hurricane

325. It lowers it

326. L. Ron Hubbard

327. Silver

328. Liquid Crystal Display

329. Halley's Comet

330. Egg white

331. Lead

332. Ammonia

333. Adam's apple

334. Gases

335. Eagle

336. Acceleration

337. Feet

338. Mercury

339. Andromeda

340. Amber

341. Copper

342. Coffee

343. Semicircles

344. A terabyte

345. The moon (John Young in the Lunar Rover)

346. The Monument

347. Acetic Acid

348. Jaundice

349. Sirius (The Dog Star)

350. Kidneys

Questions – Music

351. What singer and musician would have celebrated his eightieth Birthday on 8 January 2015 if it wasn't for his untimely death?

352. Which pop band, who had a hit with a football World Cup themed song, evolved from what had originally been Joy Division?

353. The Tamla Motown music label founded by Berry Gordy Jr began in which American City?

354. David Byrne was the lead singer in which New York based band who formed in 1975?

355. Which British band had a 1988 hit with 'Perfect'?

356. What female singer was born in Kutiasi, Georgia, before moving to Northern Ireland aged eight? She has had number one selling albums including *Call off the Search*, and *Piece by Piece*?

357. What male singer/songwriter had studio albums entitled *In Case You Didn't Know, Right Place Right Time* and *Never Been Better*?

358. Larry Adler famously played which instrument?

359. 'Rock Around the Clock' was a 1950s' hit for Bill Haley and his... what?

360. Which influential jazz musician's nickname was derived from the term 'satchel-mouth'?

361. Phil Selway, Colin Greenwood and Ed O'Brien are members of which influential rock band that formed in Oxfordshire, UK in 1985?

362. What colour was the title of R.E.M.'s sixth studio album released in 1988?

363. Sigur Ros, a post-rock band known for its falsetto vocals and ethereal sounds hail from which European country?

364. The Stratocaster is a model of guitar from which well-known guitar manufacturer?

365. *Kind of Blue* was a successful 1959 jazz album by which artist?

366. Colin Blunstone was the lead singer in which 1960s' group who had great success with their 1968 album *Odessey and Oracle*?

367. What musical that opened in the West End in 1985 features the songs 'Drink With Me', and 'Bring Him Home'?

368. Brian Warner is the real name of which controversial American musician, songwriter and actor?

369. What was the name of the Rolling Stones first record label?

370. The famous Copacabana nightclub which Barry Manilow's 1978 hit 'Copacabana' was inspired by is in which city?

371. Which song, which shares its name with a satellite, was a 1962 space-themed instrumental by British band The Tornados?

372. Which Canadian-born teen idol of the 1950s and 1960s wrote the lyrics to the song 'My Way', popularised by Frank Sinatra?

373. Who had a 1968 hit with 'Step Inside Love', written by Sir Paul McCartney?

374. Which Shakespeare character was a hit for 'Lawson' in 2013?

375. Aloe Blacc had a 2011 hit titled 'I need a...' what?

376. What partnership wrote the music and lyrics to *The King and I*?

377. In what year did The Doors front man Jim Morrison die?

378. Musician Richard Melville Hall is better known by what stage name?

379. Erasure are a synth pop duo consisting of Vince Clarke and which other singer?

380. 'Torn' and 'Shiver' were hit songs for which actress turned singer?

381. Who is credited with writing the lyrics to 'Auld Lang Syne'?

382. Matt Bellamy is the lead singer with which British rock band?

383. Who did Linda Eastman marry in 1969?

384. What group, formed in 1977, named themselves after their financial situation at that time?

385. Who sang the title theme song for the 1967 James Bond film *You Only Live Twice*?

386. Which jukebox musical is based on the formation, success and break-up of 1960s' rock 'n' roll group 'The Four Seasons'?

387. What 1978 song, written by Freddie Perren and Dino Fekaris and performed by Gloria Gaynor, received the Grammy Award for Best Disco Recording?

388. 'Skip to the good bit' by English hip-hop duo Rizzle Kicks samples which 1990 EMF song?

389. Peter Doherty and Carlos Barat are founder members of which band, that released their first studio album *Up the Bracket* in 2002?

390. 'Perfect 10' was a UK hit for which band?

391. Jazz musician Charlie Parker was most famous for playing which instrument?

392. Who is featured on Mark Ronson's single 'Uptown Funk' which spent a number of weeks at number one in both the UK and the US?

393. Johnny Cash, Jerry Lee Lewis and Elvis Presley were three members of the so-called 'Million Dollar Quartet'. Who was the fourth?

394. What dance is mentioned in both 'Bohemian Rhapsody' and 'Whiter Shade of Pale'?

395. How is American singer Katheryn Elizabeth Hudson better known?

396. What actor wrote the song 'Smile' for his 1936 film *Modern Times*. The song was subsequently covered by many well-known singers including Nat King Cole and Michael Jackson?

397. Which *Neighbours* star had a hit with the song 'Mona'?

398.   The song 'Dirty Diana' appeared on which Michael Jackson album?

399.   'Meanwhile Up in Heaven' and 'Coming Home' were singles from the studio album *Education, Education, Education & War* by which British band?

400.   What is the name of the British-American super-group consisting of Bob Dylan, George Harrison, Jeff Lynne, Roy Orbison and Tom Petty?

Answers – Music

351. Elvis Presley

352. New Order

353. Detroit

354. Talking Heads

355. Fairground Attraction

356. Katie Melua

357. Olly Murs

358. Harmonica

359. Comets

360. Louis Armstrong (Satchmo)

361. Radiohead

362. Green

363. Iceland

364. Fender

365. Miles Davis

366. The Zombies

367. *Les Misérables*

368. Marilyn Manson

369. Decca

370. New York

371. Telstar

372. Paul Anka

373. Cilla Black

374. Juliet

375. Dollar

376. Rodgers and Hammerstein

377. 1971

378. Moby

379. Andy Bell

380. Natalie Imbruglia

381. Robert Burns

382. Muse

383. Paul McCartney

384. Dire Straights

385. Nancy Sinatra

386. *Jersey Boys*

387. I will survive

388. Unbelievable

389. The Libertines

390. The Beautiful South

391. Saxophone

392. Bruno Mars

393. Carl Perkins

394. Fandango

395. Katy Perry

396. Charlie Chaplin

397. Craig McLachlan

398. *Bad*

399. Kaiser Chiefs

400. The Traveling Wilburys

Questions – Inventions and Famous Firsts

401. Sir Archibald Russell was the lead engineer in the design of which iconic aircraft?

402. It became compulsory by law to wear which device from January 1983?

403. Dentist William James Morrison invented which snack consisting of almost 100 per cent sugar?

404. Owen Maclaren helped design the Spitfire's folding undercarriage during World War II. He used his knowledge on these mechanics to produce which item now used by millions of families throughout the world?

405. What transport navigation aid was patented by Percy Shaw in 1934?

406. In 1867, Samuel B. Fay patented which frequently used stationery item?

407. Who patented vulcanised rubber in 1844?

408. Janus Friis and Niklas Zennström launched which visual messaging software in 2003?

409. *The Angel of the North*, a contemporary art piece located in Gateshead, England, was designed by which sculptor?

410. The development of what form of communication made Sir Isaac Pitman famous?

411. What did Richard Gatling invent in 1862 during the American Civil War?

412. What first appeared in *The New York World* in December 1913 and now appears in most newspapers?

413. Which commonly used fastener was invented by Walter Hunt in 1849?

414. Ruth and Elliot Handler launched which children's toy in 1959?

415. Which Danish explorer gave his name to a 'Sea', a 'Strait' and an 'Island'?

416. Who orbited the Earth for the first time in 'Vostock 1' in 1961?

417. Of which major chain of supermarkets is Jack Cohen the founder?

418. Who is credited with inventing the television in 1925?

419. Which religious organisation was founded by Joseph Smith in 1830?

420. What did Sir Christopher Cockerell invent in 1955?

421. Which American dog first appeared in a comic strip on 2 October 1950?

422. What did Howard Carter and Lord Carnarvon discover on 26 November 922?

423. What did Sir Humphry Davy invent in 1815, which aided the safety of coal miners?

424. Sir John Soane designed a building for what institution on London's Threadneedle Street?

425. Created to aid his experiments on cooling gases in 1892, what did Sir James Dewar invent that is now used by

millions every day, mainly by workmen and those enjoying the outdoors?

426. What aid to gardening was invented by Edwin Beard Budding in 1827?

427. What did Tim Berners-Lee invent in 1989 which he gave to the world for free, now used by most people every day?

428. Alexander Wood invented what medical aid in 1853 after getting inspiration from watching a honeybee sting its victim?

429. Who is credited with inventing the telephone in 1876 after gaining a patent just hours before a rival inventor?

430. William Addis, whilst in jail in 1770 saved a small animal bone from a meal and after a few adjustments, created an object, which would help the other prisoners. On his release, he mass-produced the item and set up a company named 'Wisdom'. What is the item, now used in almost every household throughout the world?

431. Powered by compressed air and an internal mechanism which enables the device to travel at a constant depth, which war aid was designed by British engineer Robert Whitehead in 1866?

432. What did twenty-four-year-old RAF fighter pilot Frank Whittle invent in 1937?

433. What did Hubert Cecil Booth invent in 1901 after watching a railway carriage being cleaned by a machine that blew the dust away?

434. In what decade of the 20th century did John Shepherd-Barron invent the ATM?

435. What is the name of the amateur chemist who in 1823 coated a thin fabric with coal-tar napthan before sandwiching it between a further two layers of fabric to make a waterproof material?

436. William Henry Fox Talbot, born in 1800 was a pioneer in the process of what?

437. Alexey Leonov was a Russian cosmonaut who was the first human to do what?

438. Which inventor, also the name of a British blues, folk and rock band invented the seed drill in 1701?

439. Who invented the wind-up radio in 1991 after seeing a television programme about Aids in Africa and the importance of education to stop its spread. The design consisted of an internal generator powered by a mainspring wind-up crank instead of needing batteries?

440. Architect Sir Christopher Wren designed and built which building on Ludgate Hill, London between 1675 and 1720?

441. Who invented a breakfast cereal named 'Granola' in 1881 before changing the name to 'Corn Flakes' after troubles with patent rights?

442. What is the name of the plumber who worked in London throughout the 19th century and held nine patents including the floating ballcock?

443. Which engineer built the first tunnel under a navigable river and the first propeller-driven ocean-going iron ship, which was at that time (1843) also the largest ship ever built?

444. What is the name of the Swedish chemist who had a synthetic element named after him and held at least 350 different patents including dynamite?

445. What piece of computer equipment was invented by Douglas Engelbart in 1963?

446. Physician to James I and Charles I, what biological system did William Harvey discover in the 17th century?

447. What did Wilhelm Conrad Rontgen discover by accident in November 1895 that made his wife exclaim 'I have seen my death' when she saw the resulting image?

448. Bernard Silver invented what revolutionary purchasing aid that was first added to a pack of Wrigley's chewing gum?

449. Which French chemist and microbiologist created the first vaccines for rabies and anthrax?

450. What did Mary Anderson patent in 1903 that was a safety device to deal with wet weather?

Answers – Inventions and Famous Firsts

401. Concorde

402. Seat belts in the front seats of a car

403. Candy Floss

404. Collapsible baby buggy

405. Cat's eyes

406. Paper clip

407. Charles Goodyear

408. Skype

409. Antony Gormley

410. Shorthand

411. The 'Gatling' machine gun

412. A crossword

413. Safety pin

414. Barbie doll

415. Vitus Bering

416. Yuri Gagarin

417. Tesco

418. John Logie Baird

419. The Mormons

420. Hovercraft

421. Snoopy

422. King Tutankhamun's tomb

423. A 'Davy' lamp

424. The Bank of England

425. Thermos flask

426. The lawnmower

427. Worldwide Web

428. A hypodermic syringe

429. Alexánder Graham Bell

430. A toothbrush

431. A torpedo

432. The jet engine

433. Electric Vacuum Cleaner

434. 1960s (1967)

435. Charles Macintosh

436. Photography

437. Space walk

438. Jethro Tull

439. Trevor Bayliss

440. St. Paul's Cathedral

441. John Harvey Kellog

442. Thomas Crapper

443. Isambard Kingdom Brunel

444. Alfred Nobel

445. The mouse

446. Circulatory/cardiovascular system

447. X-rays

448. Barcode

449. Louis Pasteur

450. Windscreen wiper

Questions – Film and Television

451. Which famous television family live at 742 Evergreen Terrace?

452. What Scottish actor played Indiana Jones' dad in the well known film franchise?

453. Who was the first black actor to receive a best actor Emmy?

454. Henry J Waternoose became the boss of which animated fictional company at the age of 142?

455. Who was the eleventh actor to play the role of the Doctor in *Doctor Who*, doing so between 2010 and 2013?

456. Which well known movie trilogy was based on a novel by Italian American author Mario Puzo?

457. Oscar-winning actress Charlize Theron was born in which country?

458. Tommy Saxondale and Tony Ferrino are characters created by which British stand up comedian and actor?

459. What actress won an Oscar for her portrayal of Leigh Anne Tuohy in the 2009 film *The Blind Side*?

460. In which sitcom might you see Compo and Clegg?

461. Who directed the award-winning film *Mystic River*?

462. Who is the tallest 'Teletubby'?

463. Which actress provides the voice of Princess Fiona in the *Shrek* film series?

464. In 1982 who was the first person to appear on Channel 4?

465. How are George Clooney, Mark Wahlberg and Ice Cube described in the title of a 1999 Iraq War film?

466. Who won an Oscar in 1959 for his role in *Ben Hur*?

467. What does the 'C' stand for in the name of the shopping channel 'QVC'?

468. What creatures were Trigger and Nutsy in Walt Disney's 1973 animated film *Robin Hood*?

469. What 1982 film ends with the title character entering his spaceship holding a geranium?

470. Which city burned in *Gone with the Wind*?

471. For which film was the promotional line 'Just when you thought it was safe to go back in the water' used?

472. What is the name of Kermit the Frog's Russian imitator in the 2014 film *Muppets Most Wanted*?

473. If James is 5, Henry is 3 and Edward is 2, who was 1?

474. Which 2014 film, directed by Morten Tyldum saw Benedict Cumberbatch portray code breaker Alan Turing?

475. What is the name of Sonny Crocket's pet alligator in the TV series *Miami Vice*?

476. What was the name of the character played by Eddie Murphy in the *Beverley Hills Cop* trilogy?

477. Which TV comedy featured characters McLaren, Blanco and Warren?

478. Film star Thomas Mapother IV is better known by what name?

479. What was Walt Disney's first feature length cartoon, released in 1937?

480. The film *Midnight Express* is set in which country?

481. On which island is *Bergerac* set?

482. Which actor has played both 'The Saint' and 'James Bond'?

483. Who played Lois Lane alongside Christopher Reeve in the 1978 film *Superman*?

484. What are the names of the two disagreeable old men, known for heckling from balcony theatre seats in *The Muppet Show*?

485. What TV contest follows twelve celebrities learning winter sports?

486. Eddie Fisher, Conrad Hilton, Jr, Mike Todd and John Warner all married which actress?

487. What is the nickname of the character who performs the 'Truffle Shuffle' in the 1985 cult film *The Goonies*?

488. What is Ennio Morricone's contribution to film and TV productions, having done so on over 500 motion pictures and television series?

489. Which TV detective comedy-drama began its broadcast in 2003 and has featured Alun Armstrong, James Bolam and Dennis Waterman amongst its cast?

490. What nationality is actor Eric Bana?

491. Which TV and film personality who died in 2014 was in the original cast of *The Mousetrap* was once chairman of Channel 4 and directed the film *Ghandi*?

492. James Norton played Sidney Chambers, an Anglican priest, in which ITV detective drama based on a series of books by James Runcie?

493. Which machine was driven by Rock and Gravel Slang in *Wacky Races*?

494. "This is Benjamin, he's a little worried about his future" was the tagline to what 1960s' film?

495. David Bradley won a BAFTA for his role as Jack Marshall in which successful TV crime drama?

496. Which member of *The Fast Show* plays the title character in *Father Brown* and also hosts TV quiz show *The Link*?

497. 'Spooky' is the look-a-like cousin of which TV and film character?

498. Morgue attendant Molly Hooper appears in which BBC detective series?

499. Which actor plays Ian Beale, the longest serving character in the BBC soap opera *EastEnders*?

500. What type of ancient monster was seen terrorising the Orient Express in a 2014 episode of *Doctor Who*?

Answers – Film and Television

451. The Simpsons

452. Sean Connery

453. Bill Cosby

454. Monsters, Inc.

455. Matt Smith

456. *The Godfather*

457. South Africa

458. Steve Coogan

459. Sandra Bullock

460. *Last of the Summer Wine*

461. Clint Eastwood

462. Tinky Winky

463. Cameron Diaz

464. Richard Whitely

465. *Three Kings*

466. Charlton Heston

467. Convenience

468. Vultures

469. *E.T. The Extra-Terrestrial*

470. Atlanta

471. *Jaws 2*

472. Constantine

473. Thomas the Tank Engine

474. The Imitation Game

475. Elvis

476. Axel Foley

477. *Porridge*

478. Tom Cruise

479. *Snow White and the Seven Dwarfs*

480. Turkey

481. Jersey

482. Sir Roger Moore

483. Margot Kidder

484. Statler and Waldorf

485. *The Jump*

486. Elizabeth Taylor

487. Chunk

488. Music composer

489. *New Tricks*

490. Australian

491. Richard Attenborough

492. *Grantchester*

493. Boulder Mobile

494. *The Graduate*

495. *Broadchurch*

496. Mark Williams

497. Casper the Friendly Ghost

498. *Sherlock*

499. Adam Woodyatt

500. A mummy

If you enjoyed this book then you might like...

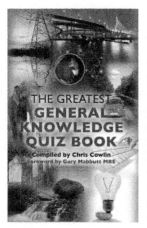

The Greatest General Knowledge Quiz Book

What does the average human head weigh? From where in the United Kingdom did the Titanic set off on her maiden voyage? Can you name the manager who took charge of the England football team in 1977? In which year did the United Kingdom first win the Eurovision Song Contest with Sandie Shaw's 'Puppet on a String'? If you can answer these questions and more like them, then The Greatest General Knowledge Quiz Book is for you.

The British TV Sitcom Quiz Book

The sitcom has proved to be one of the most enduring genres in British TV history, reflecting the social changes and national concerns of the time, and has brought many memorable and much-loved characters to our screens. Who can forget iconic figures like Frank Spencer, Basil Fawlty and Reggie Perrin or the antics of the Trotters, the Meldrews and the staff of Grace Brothers' department store, to name but a few? The 1,000 questions in The British TV Sitcom Quiz book will test your knowledge of your favourite series from yesteryear to the current day.

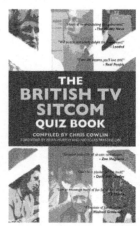